Critters and Coffee

Rebecca Kirk

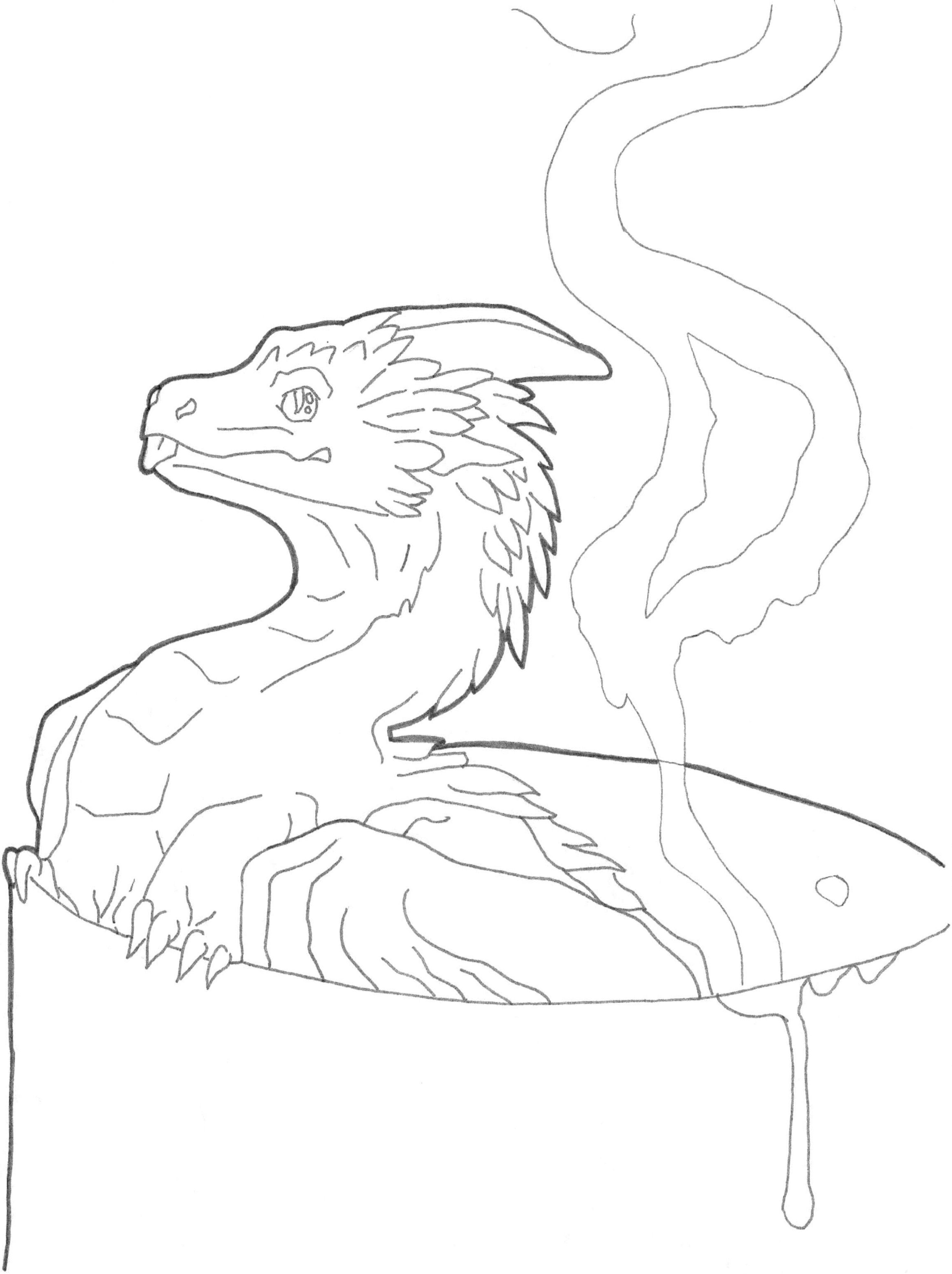

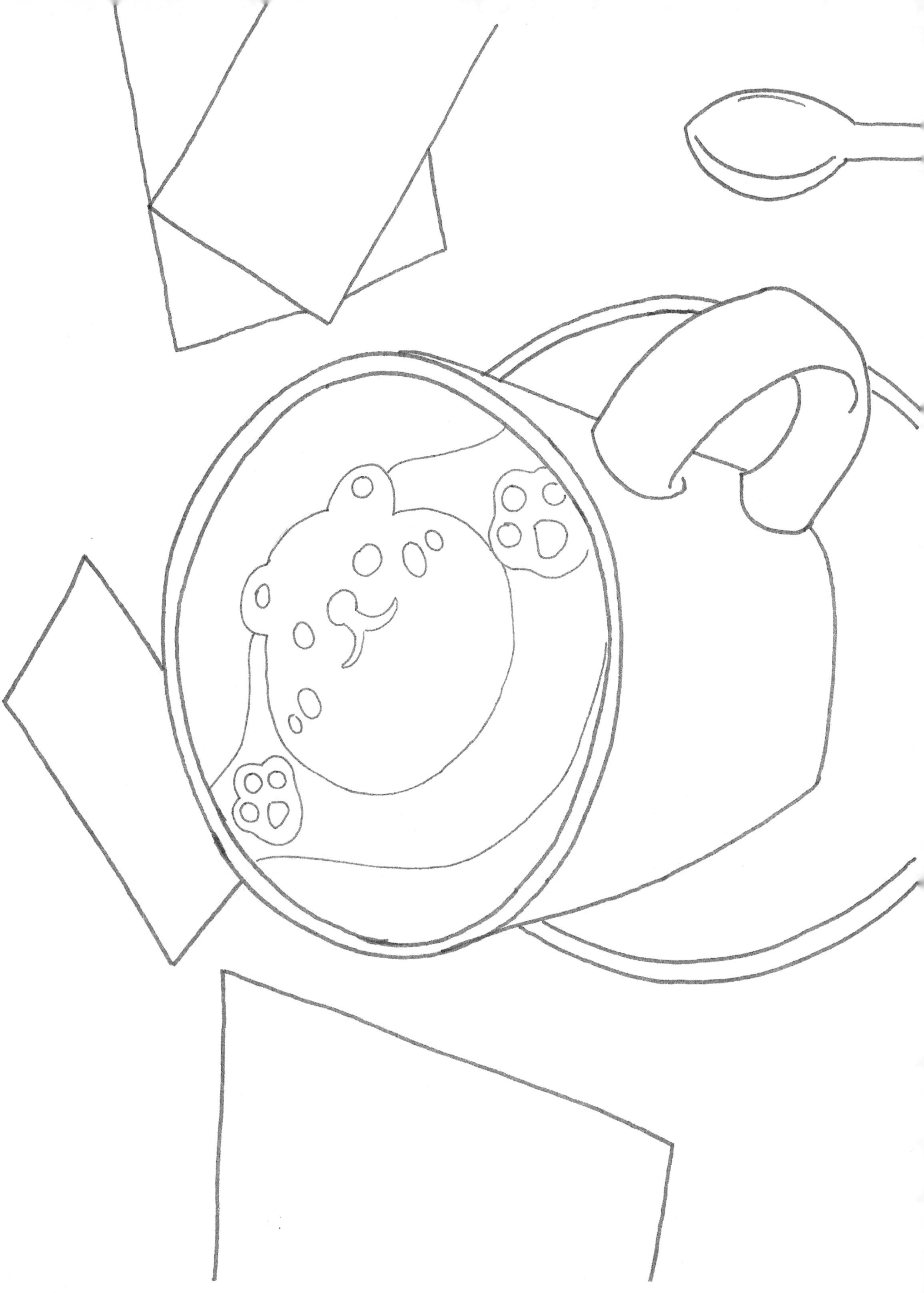

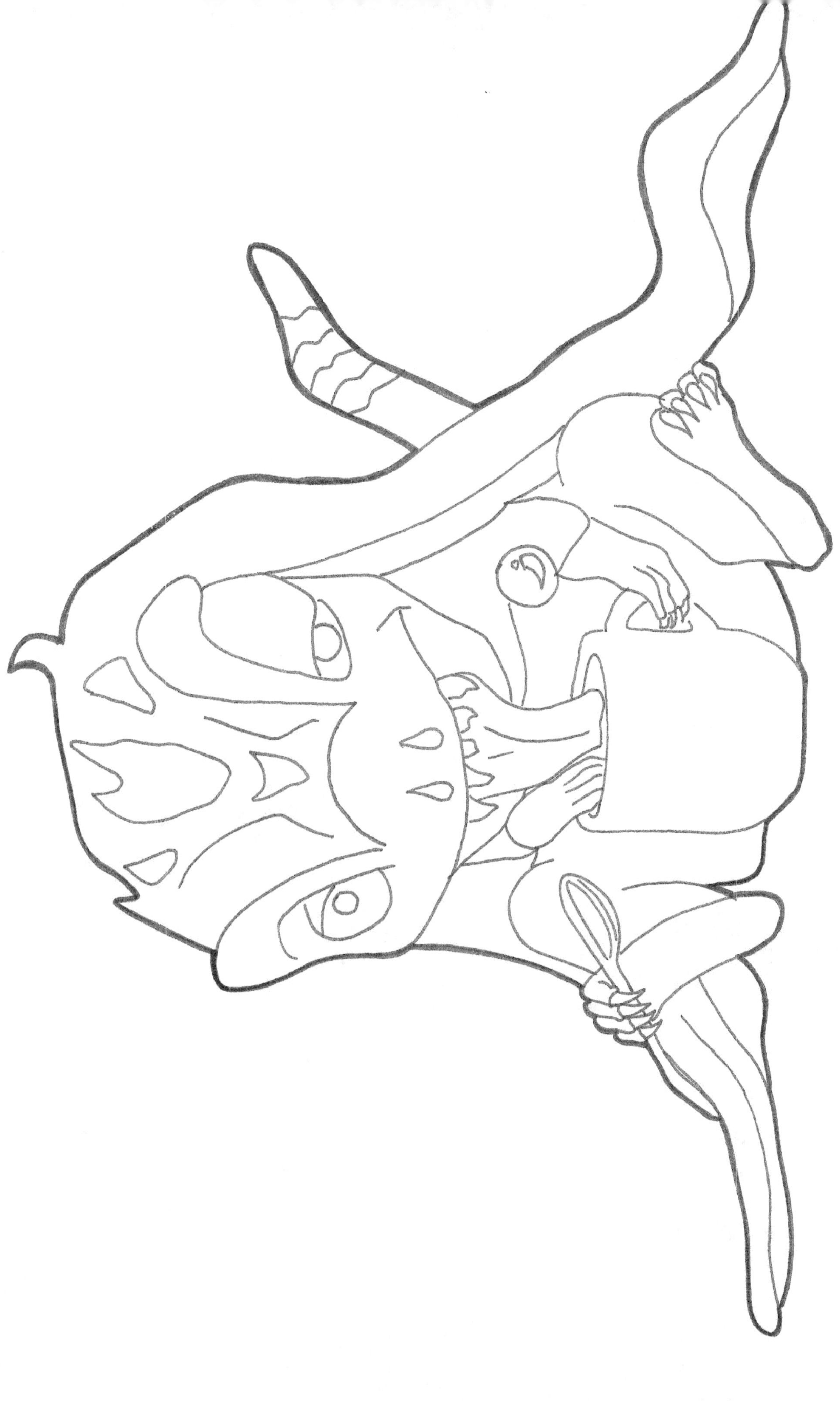

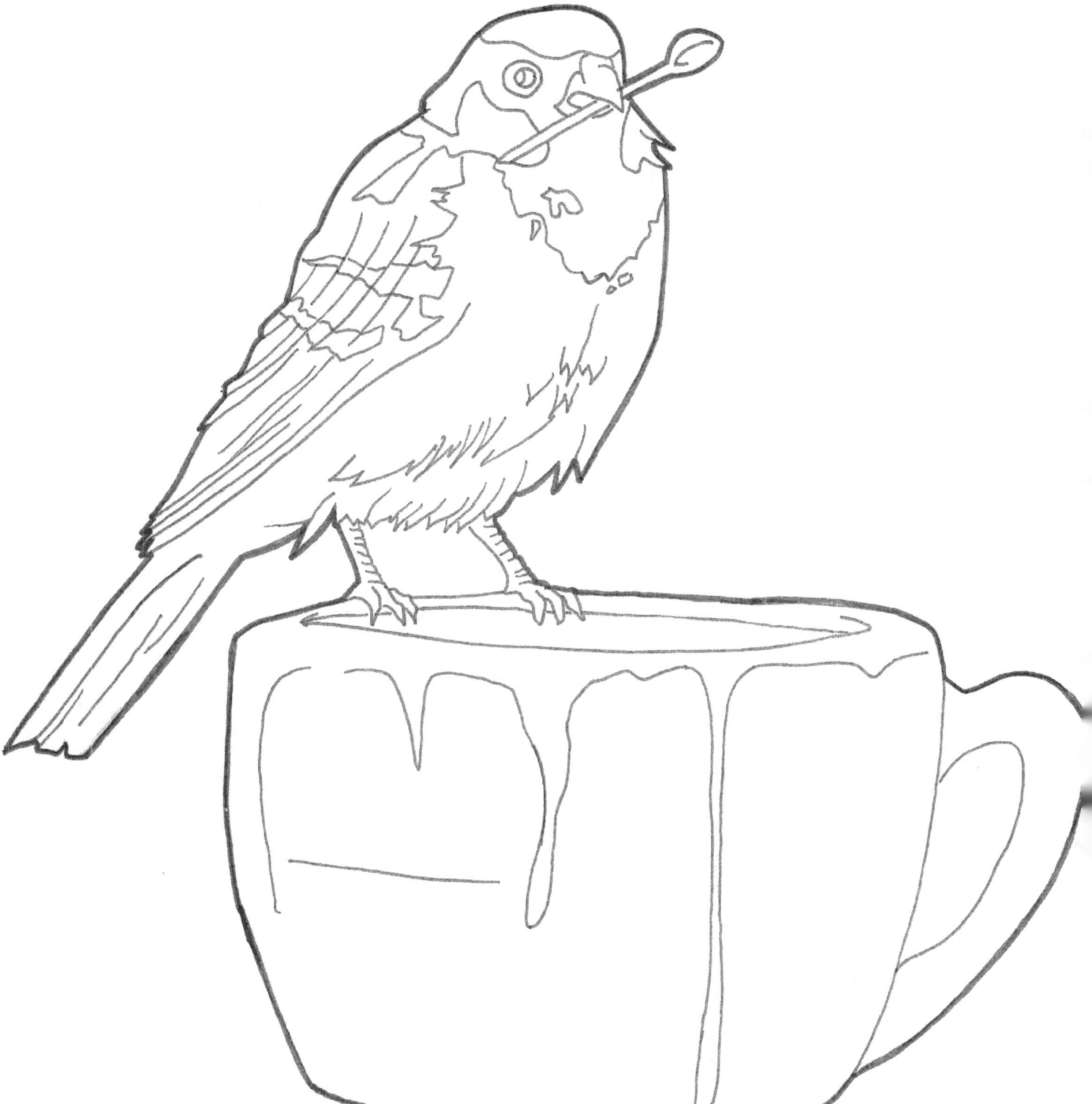

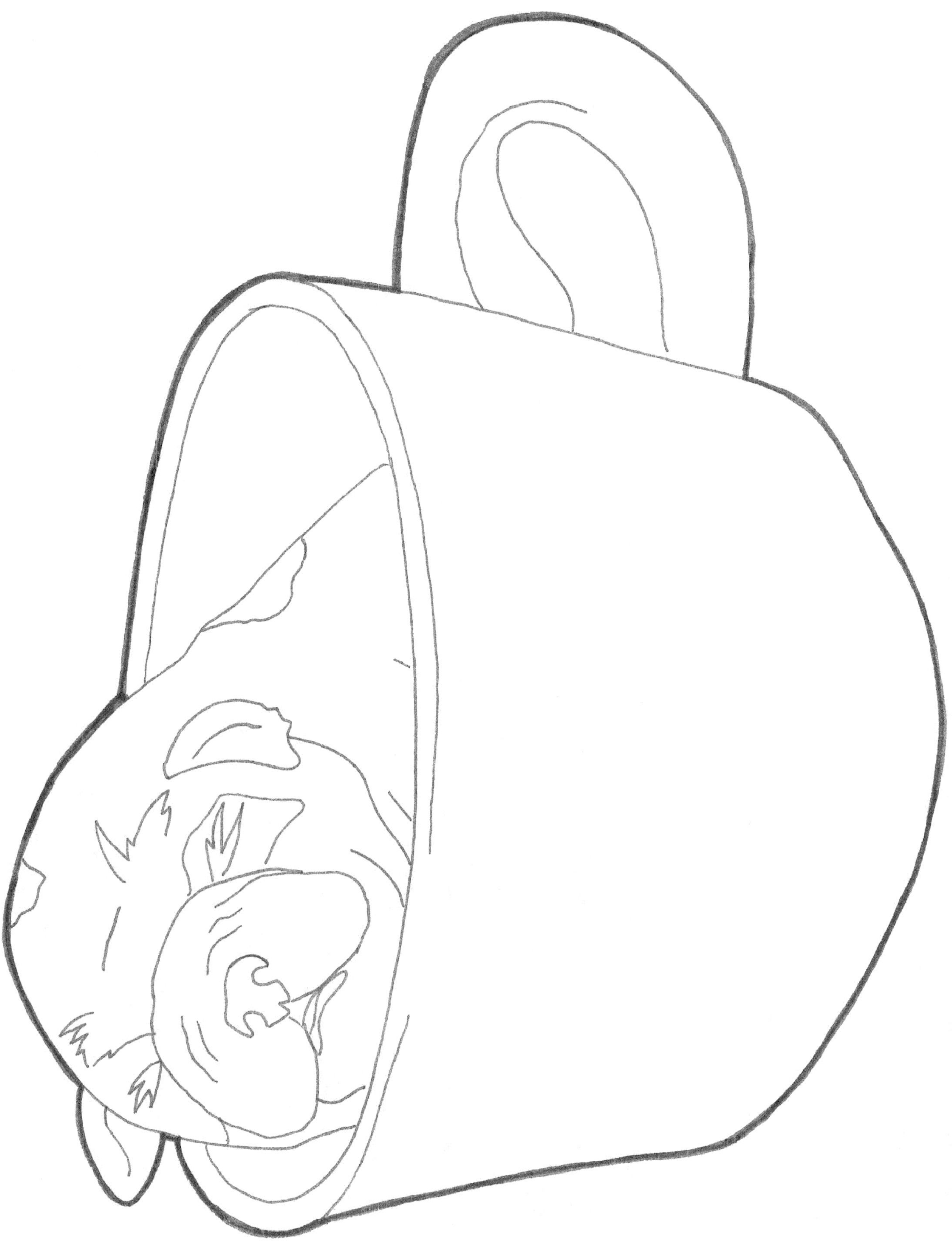

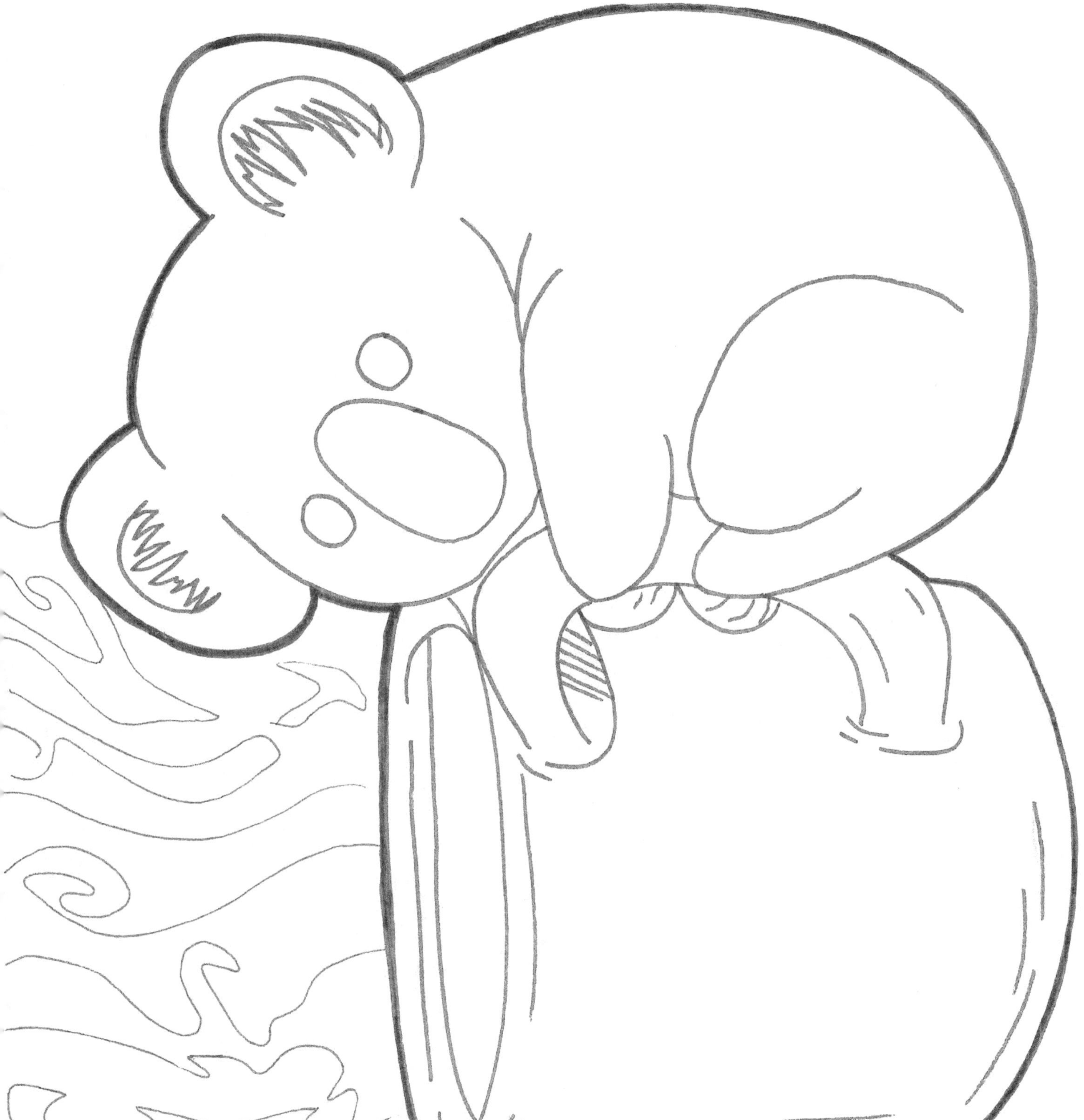

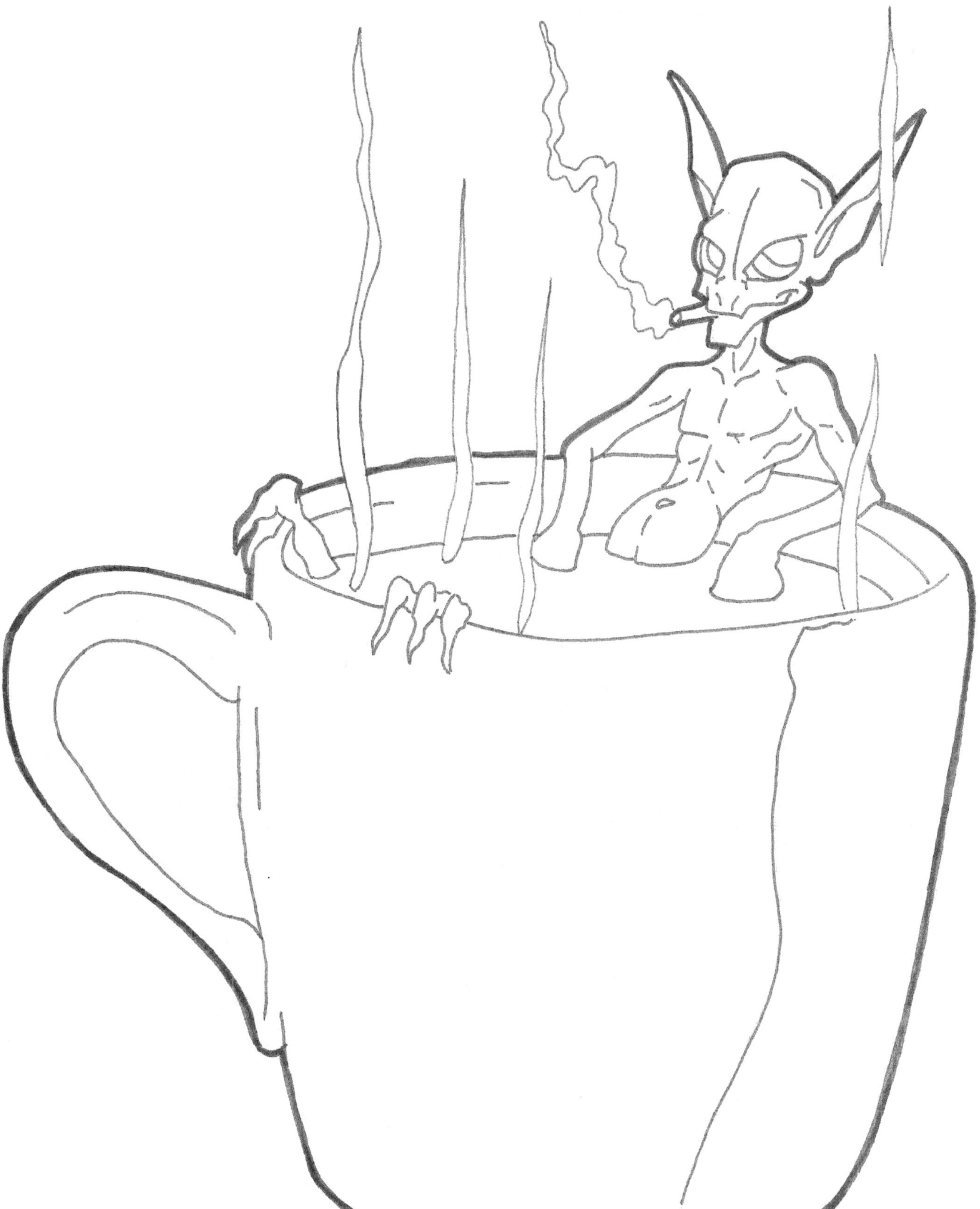

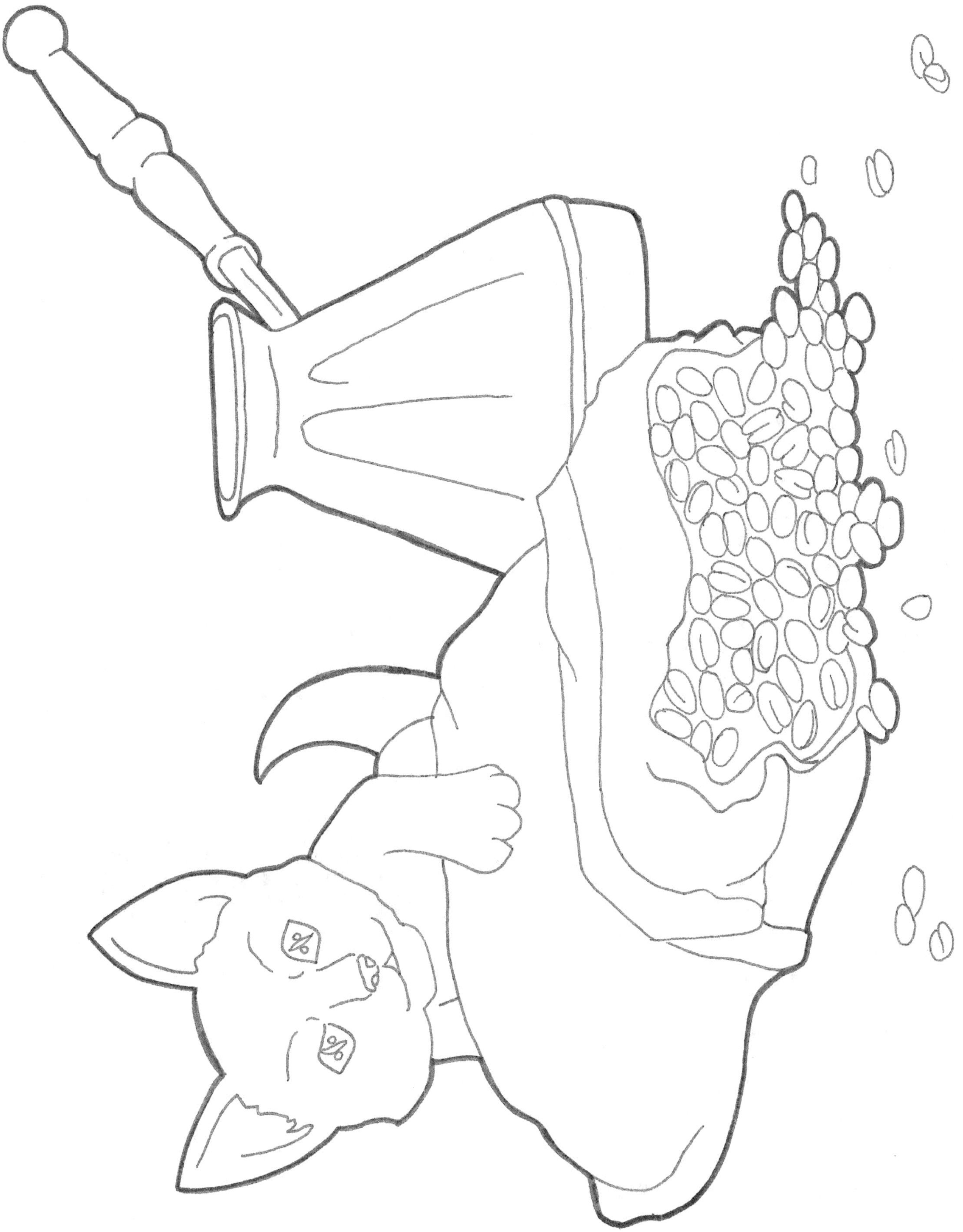

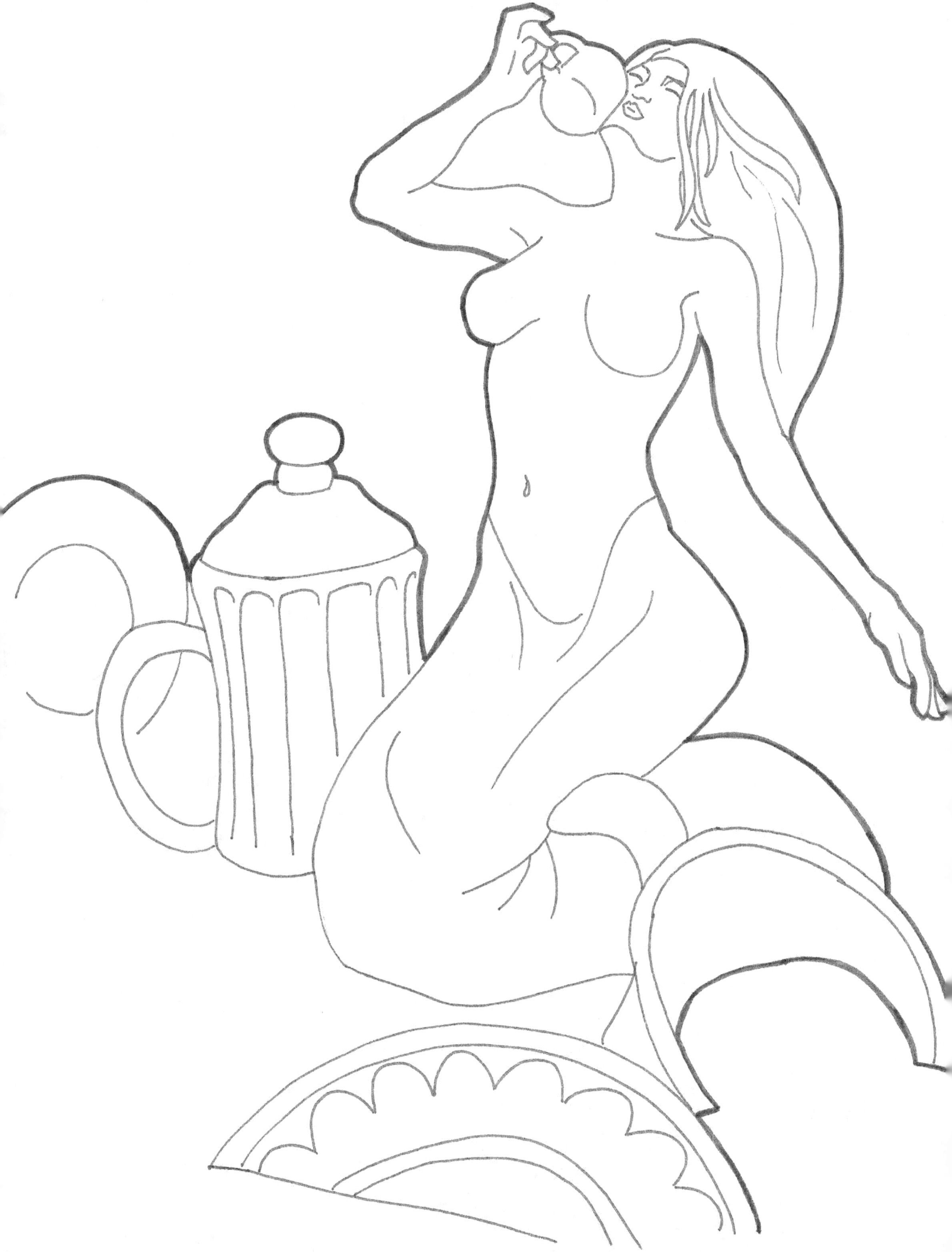

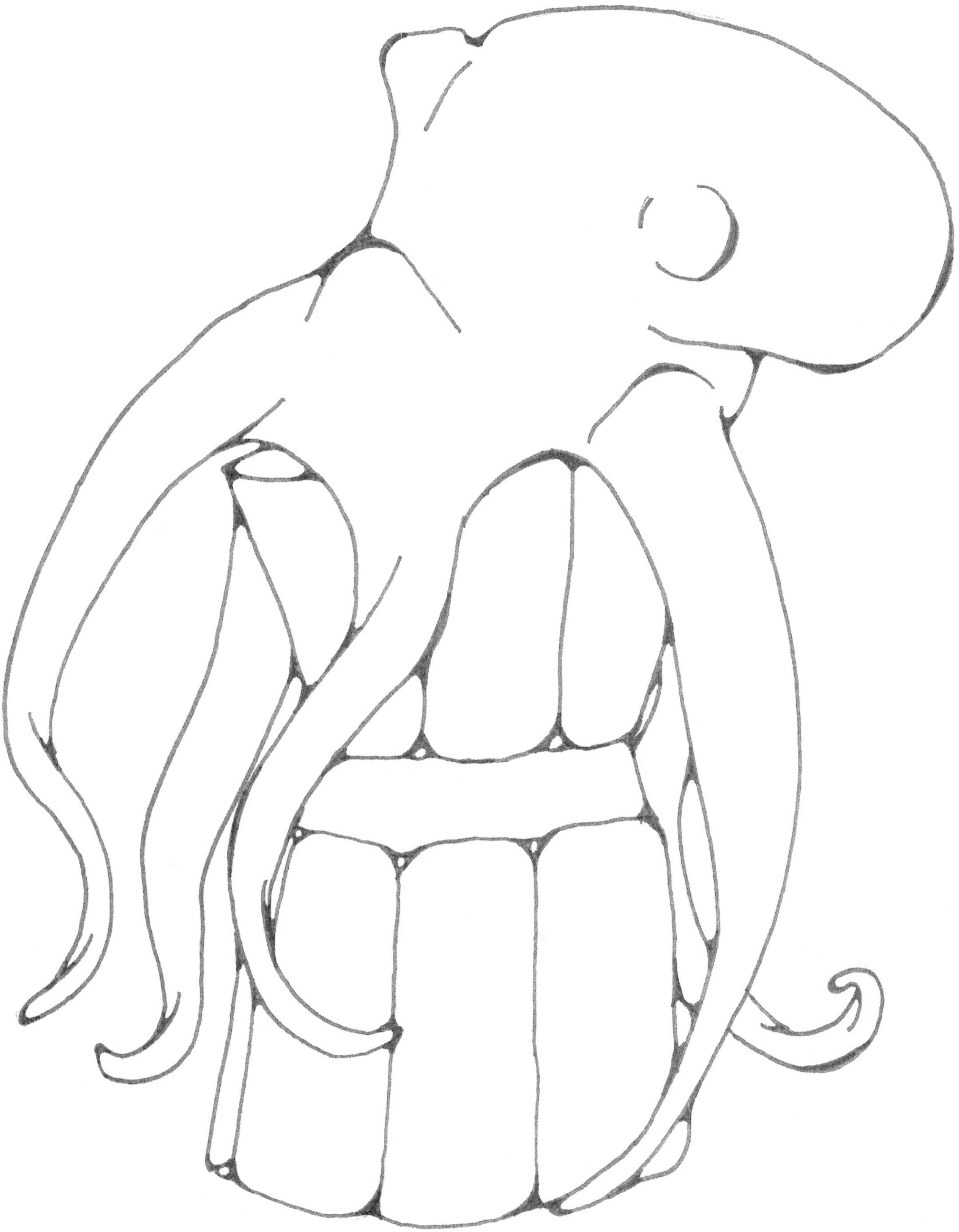

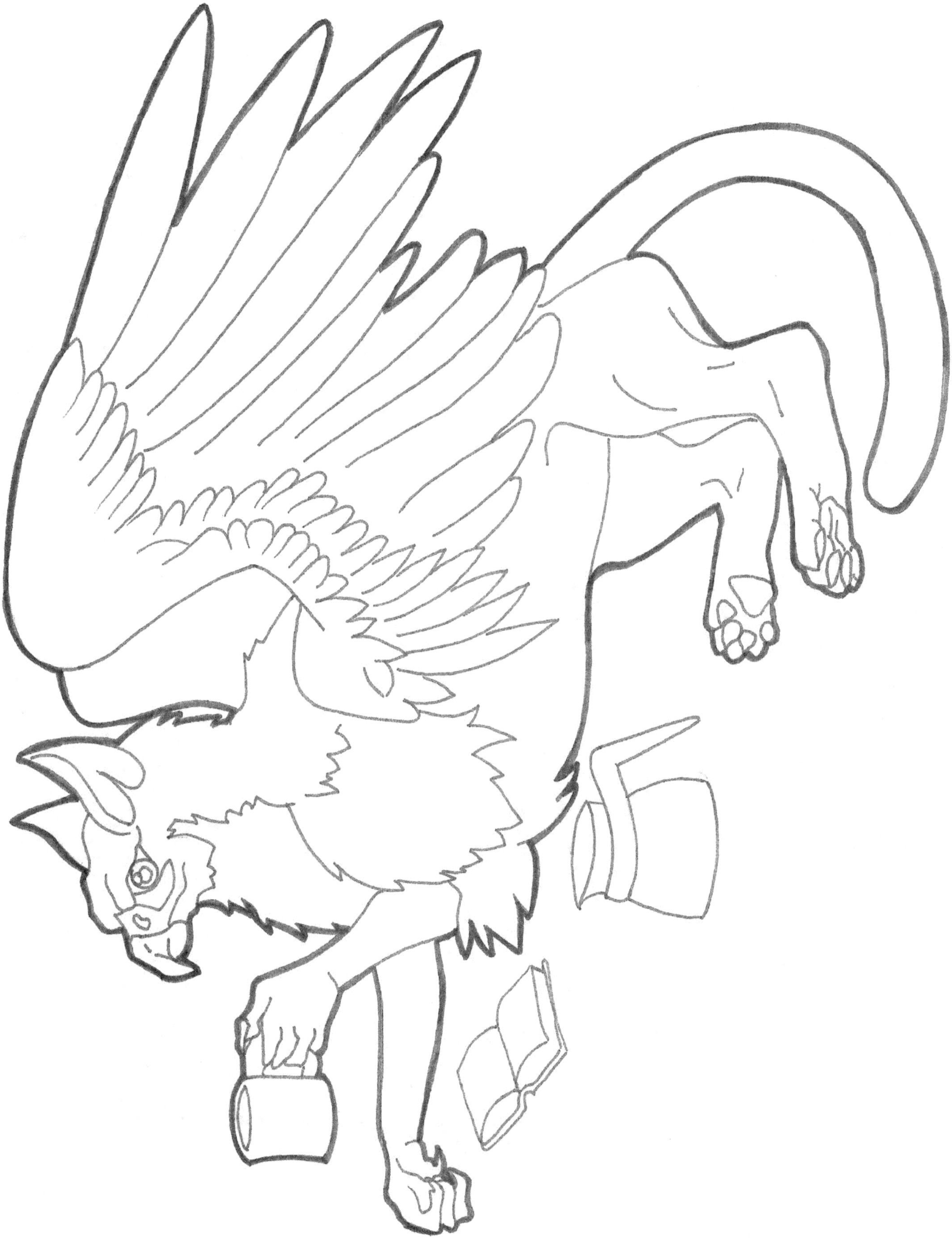

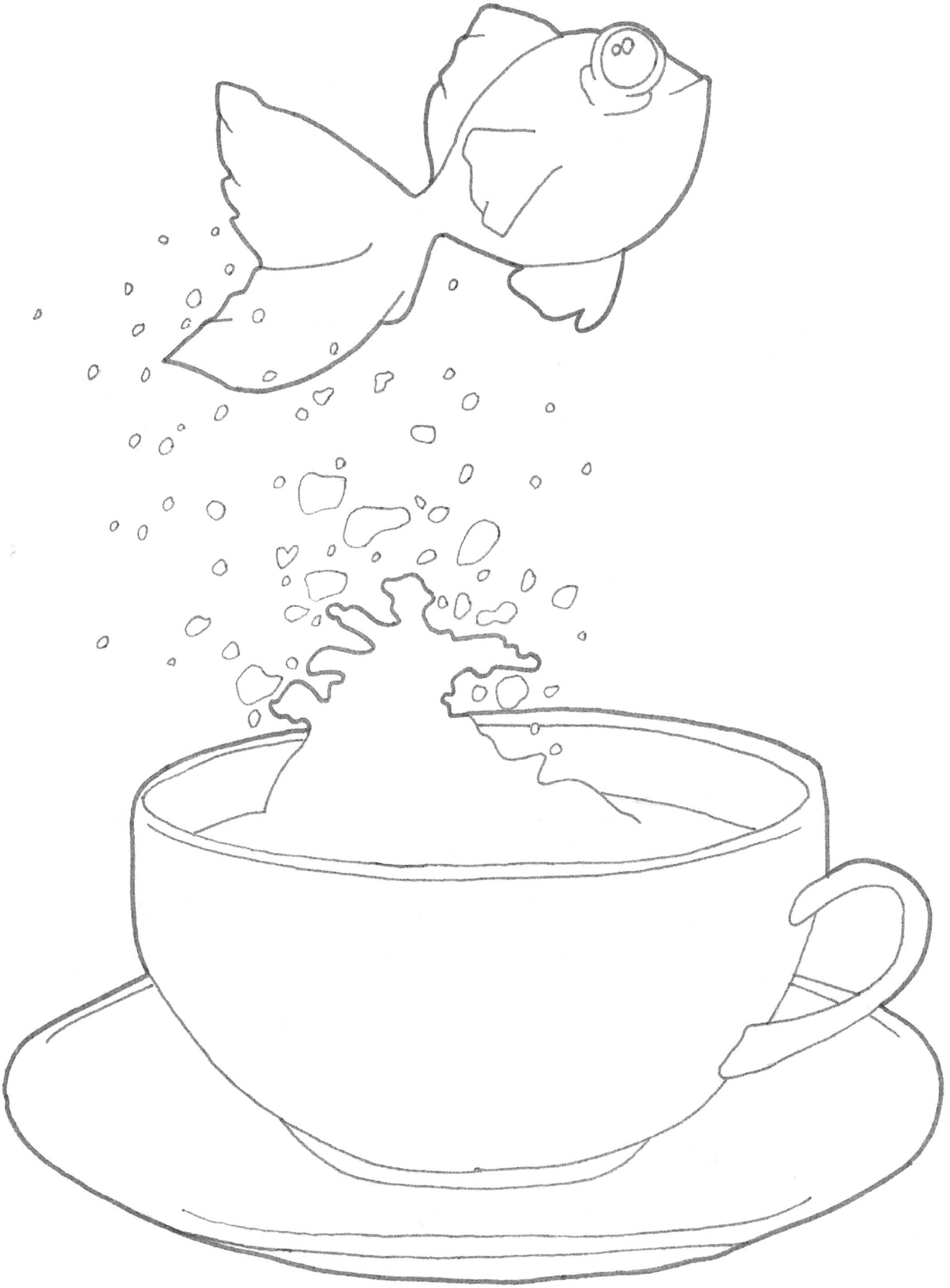

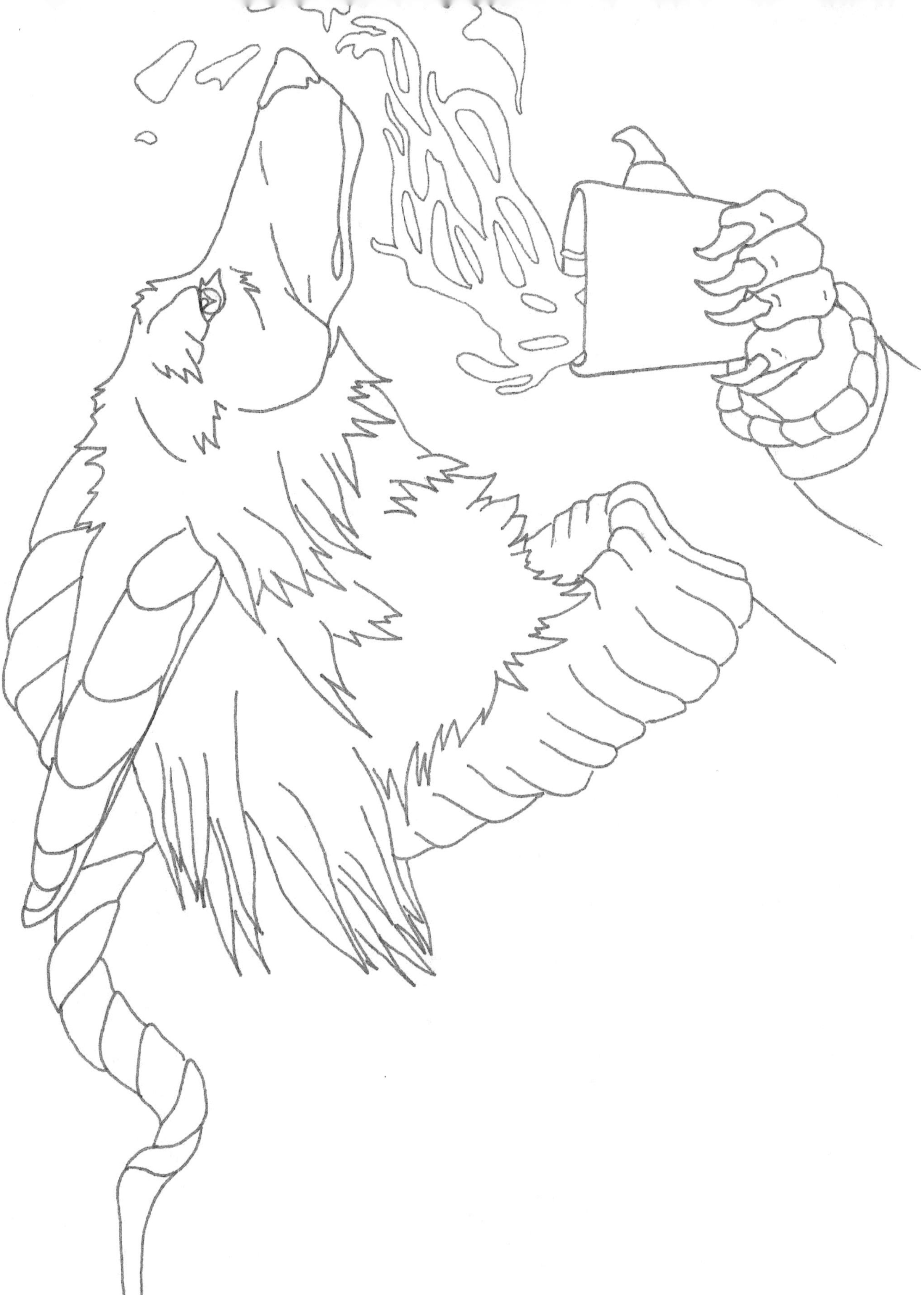

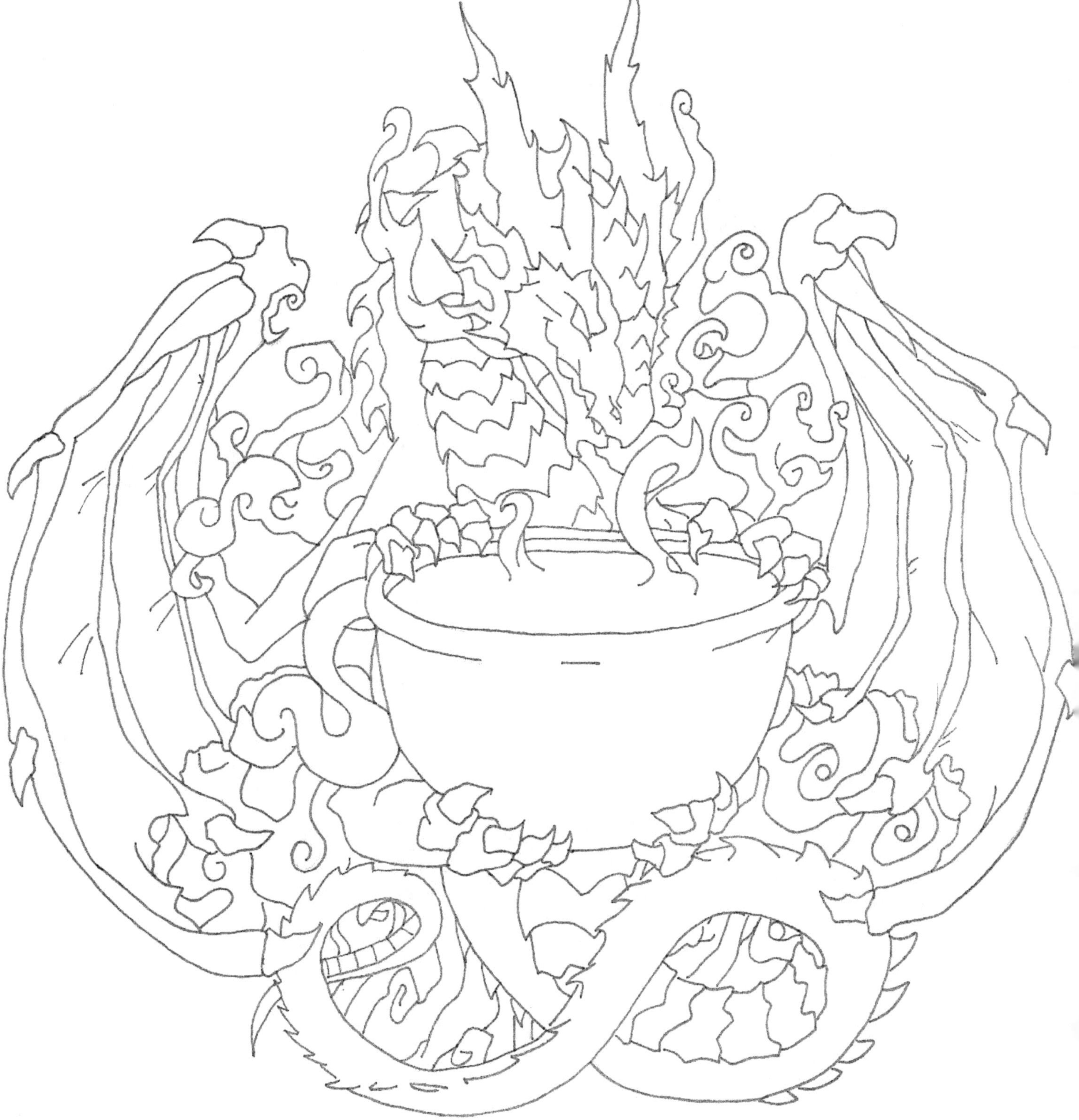

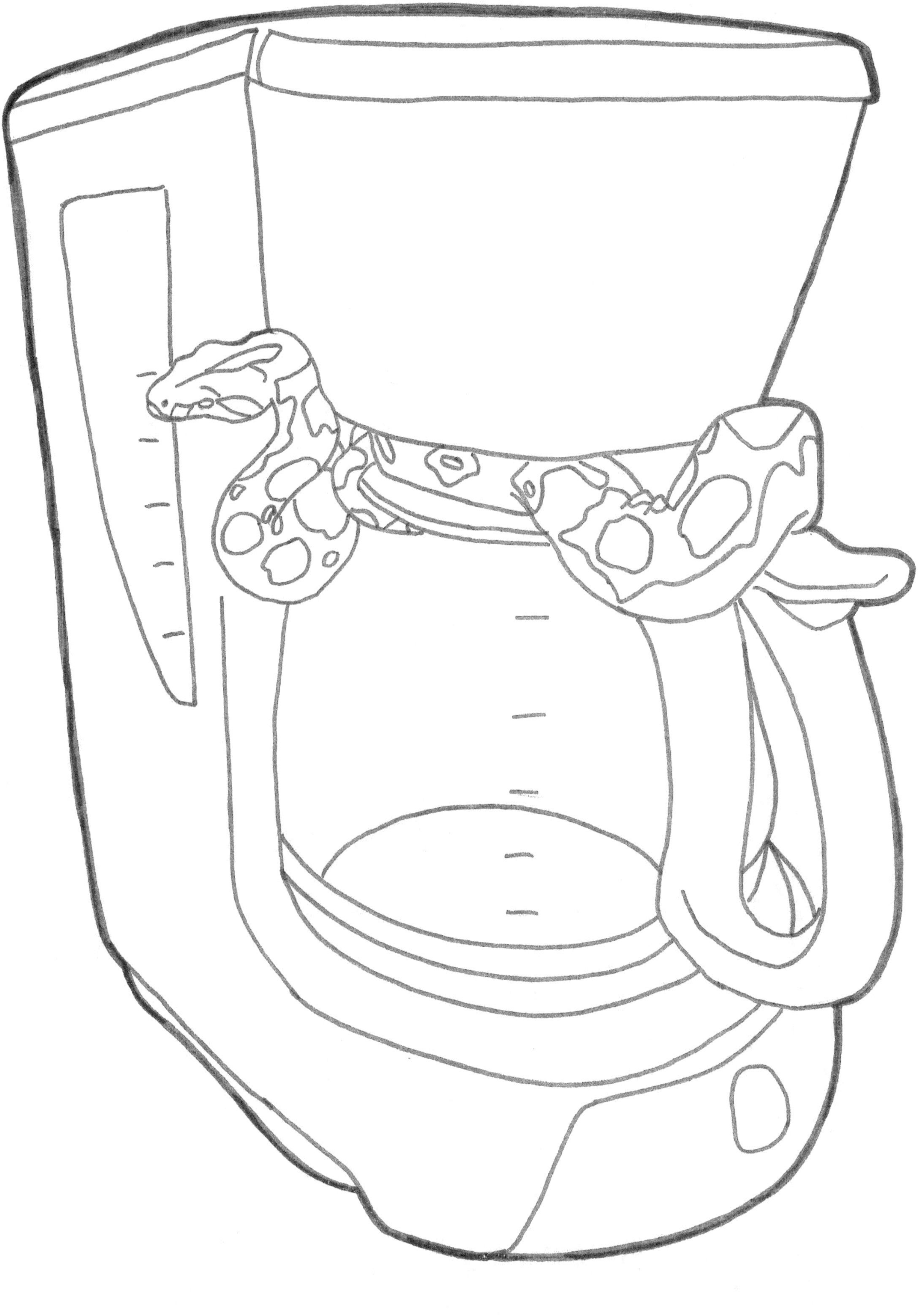

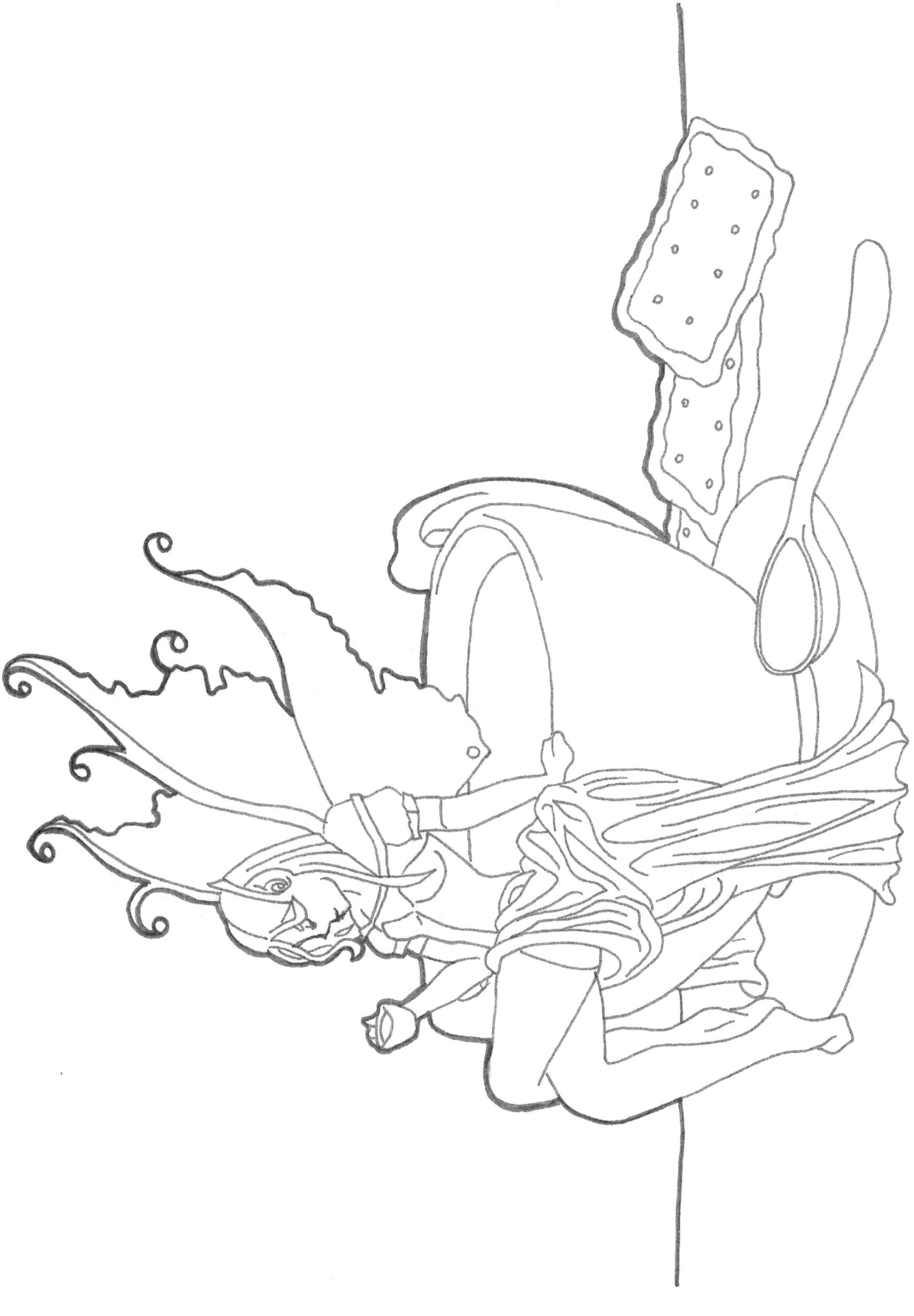

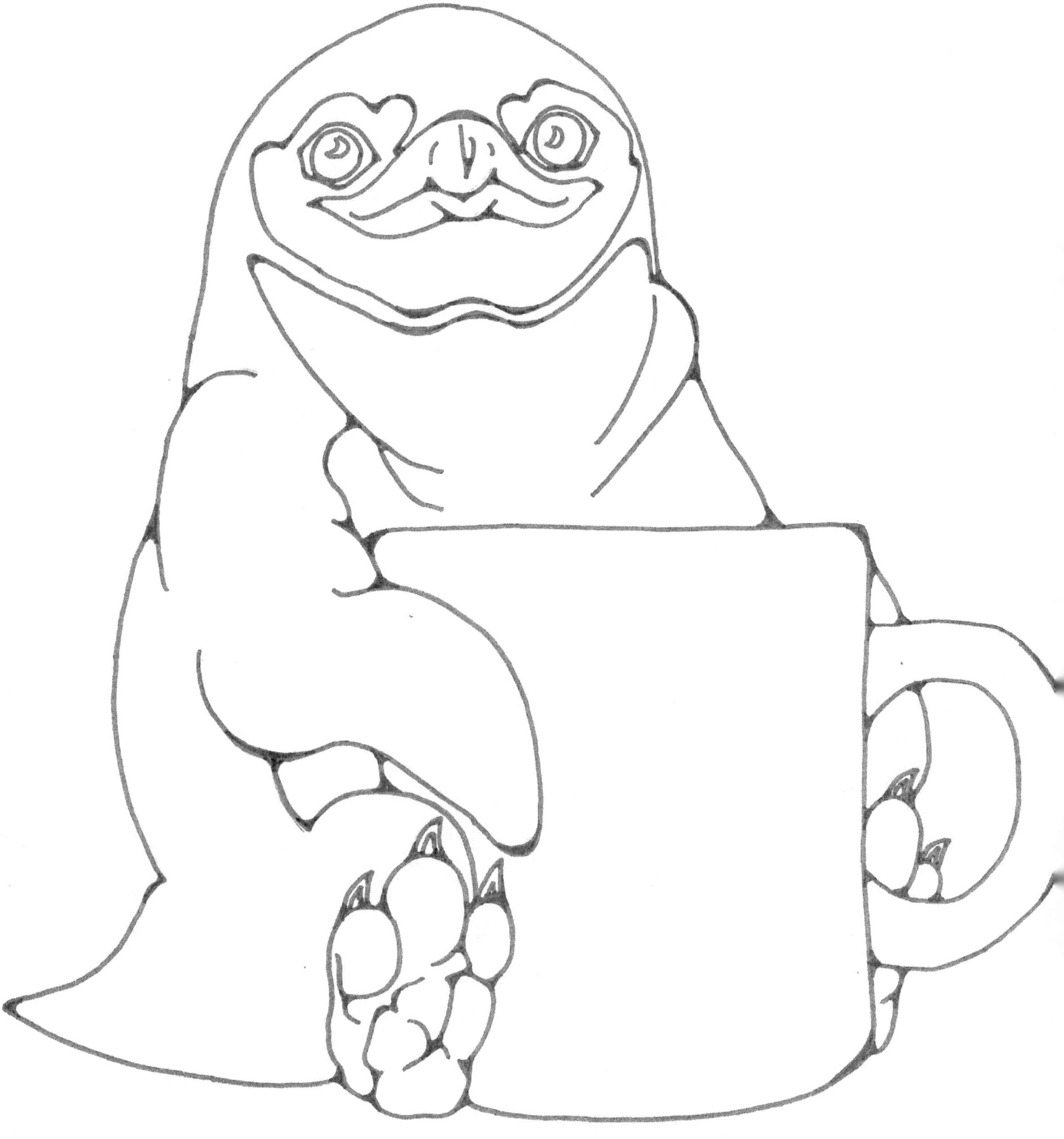

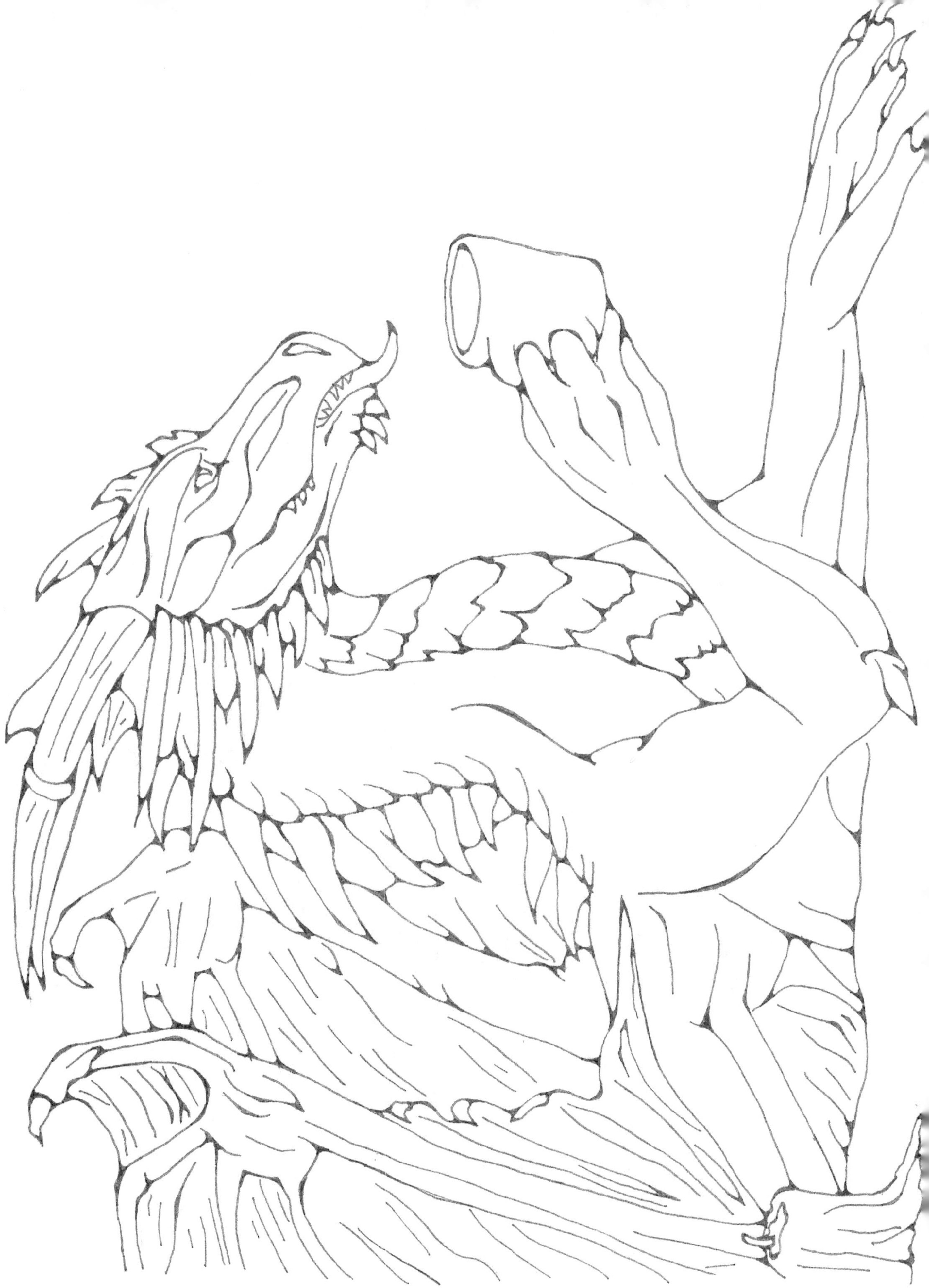

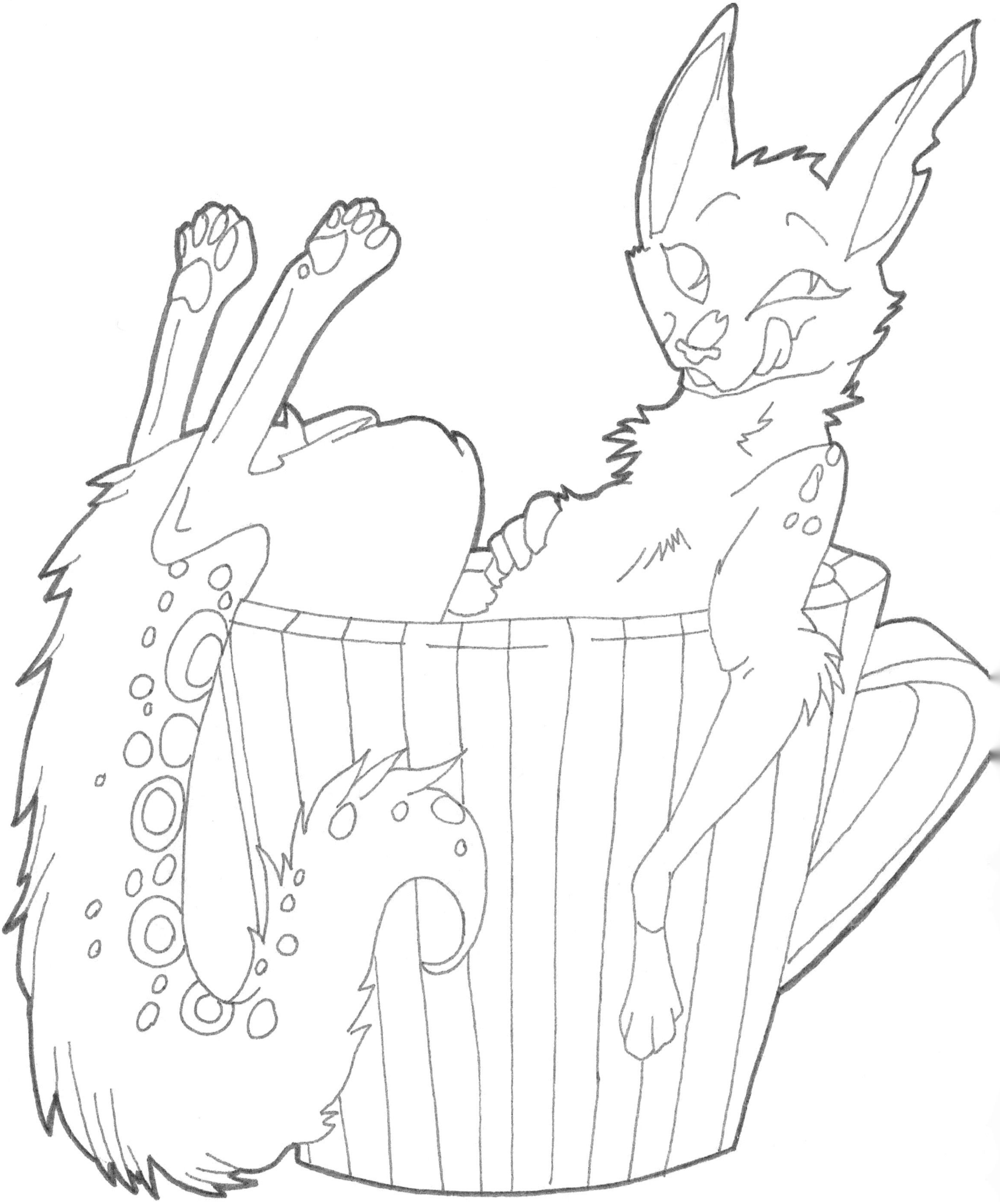

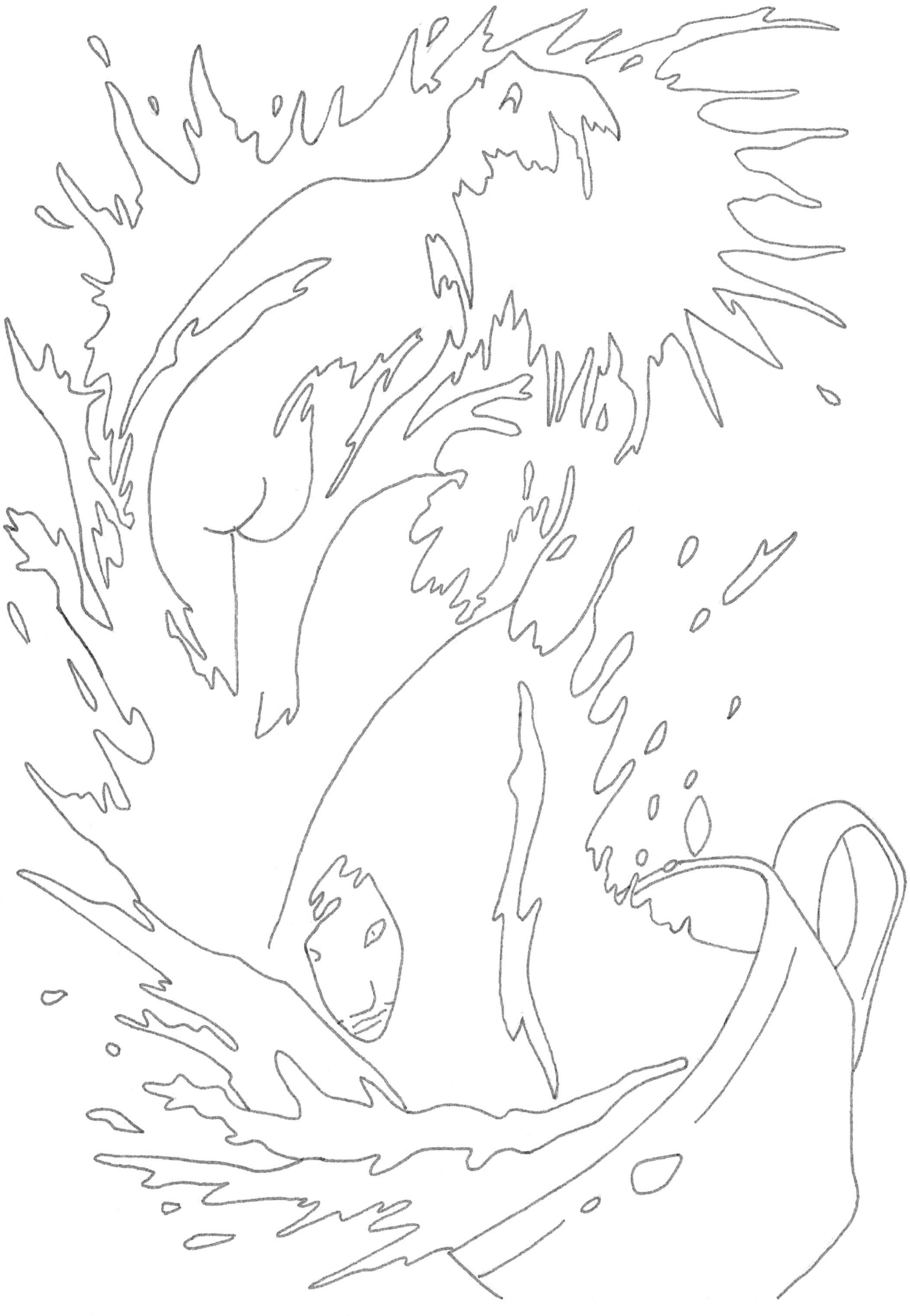

If you liked this, you might enjoy my other books

Coloring Catharsis (mature)
A Book of Many Creatures

www.ingramcontent.com/pod-product-compliance
Lightning Source LLC
Chambersburg PA
CBHW081646220526
45468CB00009B/2569